Charles M. Schulz

# *SNOOPY*
# and
# THE PEANUTS GANG

# *FIRST SERVE*

RR
Ravette London

This edition first published by Ravette Limited 1988.

Printed and bound for Ravette Limited,
3 Glenside Estate, Star Road,
Partridge Green, Horsham,
Sussex RH13 8RA
by Mateu Cromo Artes Gráfica, s.a.

ISBN: 1 85304 010 X

PEANUTS

by SCHULZ

1-4    SCHULZ

PEANUTS
by SCHULZ

CLOMP!

Hey! LET GO!!
LET GO OF
THAT MITTEN!

LET GO, I SAY!!

WOOP!

THEY SURE HAVE A LOT OF NEW THINGS
THESE DAYS FOR DOGS TO WEAR IN COLD
WEATHER..

# PEANUTS

BEAUTIFUL! JUST BEAUTIFUL!

YOU KNOW WHAT HE NEEDS? HE NEEDS SOME GLOVES!

AND AN OLD HAT! HOW ABOUT AN OLD HAT?

OUR SNOWMAN REMINDS ME OF SOME GREAT HISTORIC FIGURE!

UH HUH.. UNTOUCHED AND UNMARRED BY MODERN CIVILIZATION!

2-15

I'LL PUT UP THE WICKETS, LINUS, AND YOU POUND IN THE STAKES...OKAY?

FINE.. I ALWAYS LIKE TO TACKLE A MAN'S JOB!

WHAP WAP WHAPPITY WHAP

POW POW POW

OH, GOOD GRIEF!

?

SHEER
JEALOUSY

3-15

BOOM!

THERE'S A LESSON TO BE LEARNED HERE SOMEWHERE, BUT I DON'T KNOW WHAT IT IS...

WHAT DO YOU HAVE THERE, CHARLIE BROWN?

I'VE WRITTEN A POEM..

REALLY? READ IT..

ALL RIGHT. IT ISN'T VERY LONG..

SOME DAYS YOU THINK MAYBE YOU KNOW EVERYTHING...SOME DAYS YOU THINK MAYBE YOU DON'T KNOW ANYTHING... SOME DAYS YOU THINK YOU KNOW A FEW THINGS... SOME DAYS YOU DON'T EVEN KNOW HOW OLD YOU ARE.

THAT'S THE WORST POEM I'VE EVER HEARD!

4-19

A POEM IS SUPPOSED TO HAVE FEELING! YOUR POEM COULDN'T TOUCH ANYONE'S HEART! YOUR POEM COULDN'T MAKE ANYONE CRY! YOUR POEM COULDN'T..

WAAH!

SOME DAYS YOU THINK MAYBE YOU KNOW EVERYTHING...SOME DAYS YOU THINK MAYBE YOU..

SNIF

GOOD GRIEF!

SCHULZ

# PEANUTS
by Schulz

HI..

HI..

WHAT ARE YOU DOING THERE? YOU'RE SUPPOSED TO COLOR THE SKY **BLUE**

BLUE? THE SKY ISN'T **ALL** BLUE!

IT ISN'T?

THE SKY IS MANY COLORS..THERE'S A LITTLE BIT OF YELLOW THERE, SOME WHITE, SOME PINK, SOME GREEN AND..

**YOU'RE CRAZY!**

WELL, GO ON OUTSIDE, AND LOOK FOR YOURSELF!

ALL RIGHT, I WILL!!

WOULDN'T YOU SAY THE SKY IS BLUE, CHARLIE BROWN?

NO, I SHOULD SAY THE SKY IS MANY COLORS..THERE'S A LITTLE BIT OF YELLOW THERE, SOME WHITE, SOME PINK, SOME GREEN AND..

I OUGHTA SLUG YOU A GOOD ONE!

I DON'T EVEN KNOW WHAT'S GOING ON!!

Tm. Reg. U. S. Pat Off.—All rights reserved
Copr. 1969 by United Feature Syndicate, Inc.

5-10

DON'T LET THAT DOG LICK OFF YOUR ICE-CREAM CONE!

ARE YOU CRAZY? DO YOU WANNA GET A BUNCH OF **GERMS**? WHAT'S THE MATTER WITH YOU ANYWAY?

YOU SURE DO SOME STUPID THINGS! GOOD GRIEF!!

NOW, GO ON HOME! EAT THAT ICE-CREAM CONE YOURSELF!

I'M LESS THAN HUMAN!

6-28    SCHULZ

PEANUTS
by Schulz

DO YOU WANNA SEE A KID WITH A GREAT THROWING ARM?

THERE'S A KID WITH A GREAT THROWING ARM!

7-5

**WHAT ARE YOU DOING, LINUS?**

**I'M MAKING MY OWN SET OF FLASHCARDS**

**THESE ARE JUST LIKE THE ONES THEY USE IN SCHOOL, AND THEY'RE A GREAT AID IN LEARNING TO READ..**

**LOOOK**

**I'LL HOLD THEM UP, CHARLIE BROWN, AND WE'LL SEE HOW GOOD A READER YOU ARE... READY?**

**LOOOK**

**UH HUH!**

**VERY GOOD...NOW TRY THE NEXT ONE..**

7-19

**TAYBUL**

**GOOD. AND THE NEXT?**

**KOW**

**VERY GOOD. NOW LET'S GO A LITTLE FASTER..**

**PAYPUR, DORE, HOWSE, WELKUM, NIFE, SPUNE!**

**EXCELLENT! DO YOU WANT TO RUN THROUGH THEM AGAIN?**

**NO, I THINK ONCE IS ENOUGH...**

**AWL THYS REEDING IS HARRD ONN MI EYYS!**

SCHULZ

DEAR PENCIL-PAL,
I GUESS BY THIS TIME
EVERYBODY BUT YOU KNOWS
THAT I HAVE A BABY
SISTER.

I SHOULD HAVE WRITTEN
SOONER TO TELL YOU, BUT
I HAVE BEEN VERY BUSY.
HER NAME IS SALLY. WE
LIKE HER AND SHE
LIKES US.

OH, OH!

IN A WAY, THIS HAS BEEN
A GOOD EXPERIENCE FOR ME.
I HAVE LEARNED A LOT.
AS EVER,
CHARLIE
BROWN

SCHULZ     8-9

WHERE'S ALL YOUR STUFF, CHARLIE BROWN? WHERE'S YOUR GLOVE AND YOUR BAT AND EVERYTHING?

I CAN'T PLAY TODAY!

WADDYA MEAN, YOU CAN'T PLAY TODAY?!

JUST WHAT I SAID... I CAN'T PLAY TODAY! THERE'S SOMETHING ELSE I HAVE TO DO!!

BUT YOU'VE **GOTTA** PLAY, CHARLIE BROWN..YOU'RE OUR **MANAGER**!

YOU MAY BE A **LOUSY** MANAGER, BUT YOU'RE STILL OUR MANAGER!

WE **NEED** YOU!

I CAN'T HELP IT...

YOU GOTTA PLAY, CHARLIE BROWN!

YOU GOTTA! YOU GOTTA!

I JUST DON'T UNDERSTAND IT!

I UNDERSTAND IT!

**YOU** UNDERSTAND IT? SINCE WHEN DID **YOU** BECOME SO UNDERSTANDING?

IT'S NOT A MATTER OF UNDERSTANDING

⟪ SIGH ⟫

IT'S SIMPLY THE AGE-OLD STORY!

8-23

THUS ENDETH THE CROQUET GAME!

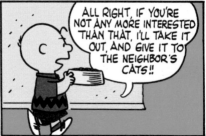

PEANUTS
by Schulz

PRETTY CLASSY!

HOW DO YOU LIKE MY NEW SHOES?

THEY'RE VERY NICE, LINUS..

SQUEAK SQUEAK SQUEAK SQUEAK SQUEAK SQUEAK

THEY KIND OF SQUEAK THOUGH, DON'T THEY?

WELL, MAYBE THEY'RE NOT PAID FOR... I'VE HEARD IT SAID THAT YOUR SHOES WILL ALWAYS SQUEAK UNTIL THEY'RE PAID FOR...

DO YOU MEAN TO TELL ME THAT JUST BECAUSE MY DAD HASN'T PAID HIS BILL, I HAVE TO WALK AROUND IN SQUEAKY SHOES?

9-27

I GUESS THAT'S RIGHT..

GOOD GRIEF!

IT'S ALWAYS THE CHILDREN WHO SUFFER FOR THE SINS OF THE MOTHER AND FATHER!

WHAT KIND OF A FOOL DO YOU TAKE ME FOR?

I'M NOT TRYING TO MAKE A FOOL OUT OF YOU...

OH, YEAH?

THE WHOLE TROUBLE WITH YOU IS YOU DON'T TRUST ANYONE!

LOOK...EVERY YEAR YOU PULL THE SAME TRICK ON ME...YOU SAY YOU'RE GOING TO HOLD THE BALL WHILE I KICK IT, BUT YOU NEVER DO!

YOU ALWAYS PULL IT AWAY, AND I LAND FLAT ON MY BACK! EVERY YEAR YOU PULL THE SAME TRICK! **EVERY SINGLE YEAR!**

LISTEN, CHARLIE BROWN, IF YOU'RE GOING TO GET ALONG IN THIS WORLD, YOU HAVE TO LEARN TO BE **TRUSTING**...

ANYONE CAN TRUST SOMEONE WHO'S TRUSTWORTHY... I'M GIVING YOU A CHANCE TO LEARN TO TRUST SOMEONE WHO IS **NOT** TRUSTWORTHY!

YOU'RE RIGHT...I'VE GOT TO LEARN TO BE MORE TRUSTING...YOU HOLD THE BALL, AND I'LL KICK IT...

10-4

SHE DID IT AGAIN!

WUMMS!

SEE YOU HERE AGAIN NEXT YEAR?

Tm. Reg. U. S. Pat Off.—All rights reserved
Copr. 1959 by United Feature Syndicate, Inc.

SCHULZ

**PEANUTS** by CHARLES M. SCHULZ

*Bread*

CHOMP CHOMP

CHOMP CHOMP CHOMP

CHOMP CHOMP

HANDS ARE FASCINATING THINGS!

I LIKE MY HANDS..I THINK I HAVE NICE HANDS...

MY HANDS SEEM TO HAVE A LOT OF CHARACTER...

THESE ARE HANDS WHICH MAY SOMEDAY ACCOMPLISH GREAT THINGS...THESE ARE HANDS WHICH MAY SOMEDAY DO MARVELOUS WORKS!

THEY MAY BUILD MIGHTY BRIDGES, OR HEAL THE SICK, OR HIT HOME-RUNS, OR WRITE SOUL-STIRRING NOVELS!

THESE ARE HANDS WHICH MAY SOMEDAY CHANGE THE COURSE OF DESTINY!

THEY'VE GOT JELLY ON THEM!

10-11

SCHULZ

IT ALWAYS COMES AS A SHOCK WHEN IT HAPPENS TO SOMEONE YOU KNOW...

SMACK!

ZIP!

IF YOU CAN'T TRUST DOGS AND LITTLE BABIES, WHOM CAN YOU TRUST?

**PEANUTS** by SCHULZ

SO THERE, TOO!!

NYAHH!!

NYAHH, NYAHH, NYAHH, NYAHH!

IF YOU SAY THAT TO ME ONCE MORE, I'M GONNA SLUG YOU!

YOU CAN'T SLUG ME, LINUS, BECAUSE I'M A GIRL! **NYAHH!!**

WELL, BY GOLLY, I CAN SURE THROW A ROCK AT YOU! WHERE'S A ROCK? JUST LET ME FIND A GOOD ROCK...

HOLD ON THERE! YOU CAN'T THROW A ROCK AT A GIRL! ARE YOU CRAZY OR SOMETHING?

HOW ABOUT A TENNIS BALL? WHERE'S A TENNIS BALL? I'LL HIT HER WITH A TENNIS BALL! THAT'LL JUST **STING** A LITTLE..

NO, YOU CAN'T HIT HER WITH A TENNIS BALL EITHER!

HOW ABOUT A PING PONG BALL?

NO! YOU CAN'T HIT A GIRL WITH ANYTHING! YOU CAN'T EVEN THINK ABOUT HITTING A GIRL! **THINKING** ABOUT IT IS JUST AS BAD AS DOING IT!

CAN I SAY "NYAHH" BACK AT HER?

NO, YOU CAN'T DO THAT EITHER!

Tm. Reg. U. S. Pat Off.—All rights reserved
Copr. 1959 by United Feature Syndicate, Inc.

HOW WOULD IT BE IF I SLUG **YOU**?

11-8     SCHULZ

**PEANUTS** by Schulz

HERE'S THE FIERCE MOUNTAIN LION SNEAKING THROUGH THE GRASS...

HERE'S THE AGILE MOUNTAIN LION BOUNDING THROUGH THE UNDERBRUSH.

HERE'S THE PROUD MOUNTAIN LION SITTING ATOP A ROCK...

11-29

SUDDENLY HE SEES AN APPROACHING FIGURE!

HE CROUCHES BEHIND THE ROCK...

HE LEAPS!!

GROARR!

RIP! SNARL! TEAR!

POUNCE POUNCE POUNCE POUNCE

Tm. Reg. U. S. Pat Off.—All rights reserved
Copr. 1969 by United Feature Syndicate, Inc.

SIGH

DEAR PENCIL PAL,
ON MY WAY HOME FROM SCHOOL TODAY I WAS ATTACKED BY A MOUNTAIN LION. I WAS NOT SERIOUSLY INJURED.

Schulz

YOU KNOW, I CAN'T POSSIBLY TELL YOU HOW SICK I GET OF SEEING YOU DRAG AROUND THAT STUPID BLANKET!

IT'S NOT STUPID... THIS BLANKET HAS MANY VERY PRACTICAL USES...

HA! THAT'S A LAUGH!

YOU JUST HAVE NO IMAGINATION, THAT'S ALL

I HAVE PLENTY IMAGINATION... IT DOESN'T TAKE ANY IMAGINATION TO SEE HE'S **CRAZY!**

OF ALL THE BROTHERS IN THE WORLD, I HAD TO GET **HIM!**

WELL, YOU'LL HAVE TO ADMIT HE'S DONE IT AGAIN!

HUH?

I SAID LINUS HAS DONE IT AGAIN..YOU'D BETTER GO SEE FOR YOURSELF...

12-6

HOLD THE BLANKET IN YOUR LEFT HAND...THAT'S THE WAY...

PEANUTS by SCHULZ

NOW THE THUMB...

WHAT IN THE WORLD IS GOING ON HERE?!

LOOK, LINUS, YOU'RE NOT GONNA TEACH ANY SISTER OF MINE TO SIT AROUND HOLDING A BLANKET!

JUST BECAUSE YOU NEED A CRUTCH, IT DOESN'T MEAN SHE DOES!

OF ALL THE STUPID HABITS, THAT BLANKET IS THE STOPIDEST! AND THAT'S ALL IT IS, JUST A HABIT! A STUPID HABIT!!

YOU'RE NOT GOING TO TEACH HER TO USE A BLANKET FOR SECURITY OR FOR HAPPINESS OR FOR ANYTHING! SALLY IS GOING TO USE HER OWN WILL-POWER TO GROW FROM A BABY TO A WELL-ADJUSTED CHILD !!!!

LIKE HER BROTHER?

3-20

SIGH

I'M GOING HOME TO EAT LUNCH, SNOOPY, AND I WANT YOU TO GUARD MY SNOWMAN.. DON'T LET ANYONE HARM IT!

ONE THING I'M GOOD AT IS GUARDING THINGS! IT'S A POINT OF DISTINCTION WITH MY PARTICULAR BREED!

I'LL GUARD THIS SNOWMAN AGAINST ENEMIES FROM THE NORTH, SOUTH, EAST AND WEST! I'LL GUARD THIS SNOWMAN AGAINST ENEMIES FROM BELOW AND FROM...

.......above........

YOU JUST CAN'T DO ANYTHING, CAN YOU?

1-17

**HOLD IT!!**

IS THIS ALL YOU HAVE TO DO? ARE YOU GOING TO SPEND THE WHOLE DAY SLIDING BACK AND FORTH ON A PIECE OF ICE?!

DO YOU THINK THESE DAYS WERE GIVEN TO YOU TO WASTE? DOESN'T LIFE MEAN MORE TO YOU THAN THIS?!

1-31    SCHULZ

FIVE O'CLOCK...TIME TO FEED THE DOG..

OKAY, SNOOPY... HERE YOU ARE...

OH, IT'S SUPPERTIME! IT'S SUPPERTIME!

SUPPERTIME! SUPPERTIME! SUPPERTIME!!

HEY! CUT IT OUT - NOW! WATCH WHAT YOU'RE DOING!

OH, IT'S SUPPERTIME! IT'S SUPPERTIME!!

YES, IT'S SUPPERTIME!

OH, YES, YES, YES, YES, IT'S SUPPERTIME! IT'S SUPPERTIME! IT'S...

ALL RIGHT, EAT!

GOOD GRIEF!

Tm. Reg. U. S. Pat. Off.—All rights reserved
Copr. © 1959 by United Feature Syndicate, Inc.

SO WHAT'S WRONG WITH MAKING MEALTIME A JOYOUS OCCASION?

12-13                    SCHULZ

**PEANUTS** by SCHULZ

YES, SIR... LONG PANTS SURE DO MAKE THE MAN!

WELL, HOW DO I LOOK?

FINE...IT'S THE FIRST TIME I'VE SEEN YOU IN A WHITE SHIRT IN SIX MONTHS!

NOW ARE YOU SURE YOU KNOW YOUR PIECE FOR THE CHRISTMAS PROGRAM?

I KNOW IT BACKWARDS AND FORWARDS AND SIDEWAYS AND UPSIDE DOWN! I COULD SAY IT IN MY SLEEP!

YEAH, WELL, I REMEMBER **LAST** YEAR..YOU ALMOST GOOFED THE WHOLE PROGRAM!

WELL, THIS IS **THIS** YEAR, AND **THIS** YEAR I WON'T FORGET!

"AND THE ANGEL SAID UNTO THEM, FEAR NOT: FOR, BEHOLD, I BRING YOU GOOD TIDINGS OF GREAT JOY WHICH SHALL BE TO ALL PEOPLE."

SAY, THAT'S PRETTY GOOD.

I **TOLD** YOU I KNEW IT.. I HAVE A MEMORY LIKE THE PROVERBIAL ELEPHANT!

WELL, I'M GOING ON AHEAD TO THE CHURCH...I'LL SEE YOU THERE...

"...FOR, BEHOLD, I BRING YOU GOOD TIDINGS OF GREAT JOY WHICH SHALL BE TO ALL PEOPLE." WHAT A MEMORY!!!

12-20

WHAT IN THE WORLD? I THOUGHT YOU JUST LEFT?

I DID, BUT I CAME BACK..

I FORGOT WHERE THE CHURCH IS!

SCHULZ

# PEANUTS
## by SCHULZ

**CLOMP**

WHEN!

ARE YOU CRAZY? IT'S COLD OUTSIDE! YOU COULD CATCH PNEUMONIA ROLLING AROUND OUT THERE IN THE SNOW!

THE STRUGGLE FOR SECURITY KNOWS NO SEASON!

1-10

HI, SNOOPY...HI SHERMY...GLAD YOU MADE IT.. HI, PIG-PEN...

HI, VIOLET...HOW'S THE WORLD'S PRETTIEST THIRD BASEMAN? HI, LINUS...HI, LUCY...

HI, PATTY...HI, SCHROEDER...HOW'S THE OL' THROWIN' ARM?

PEANUTS by SCHULZ

WELL, IT'S REAL GOOD SEEING YOU ALL HERE READY TO BEGIN THE NEW BASEBALL SEASON...

DUE TO THE RAIN TODAY, WE WILL FOLLOW THE INCLEMENT WEATHER SCHEDULE...THIS MEANS STUDYING OUR SIGNALS..

NOW A GOOD BASEBALL TEAM FUNCTIONS ON THE KNOWLEDGE OF ITS SIGNALS. THIS YEAR WE WILL TRY TO KEEP THEM SIMPLE...

IF I TOUCH MY CAP LIKE THIS, IT MEANS FOR WHOEVER HAPPENS TO BE ON BASE TO TRY TO STEAL..

IF I CLAP MY HANDS, IT MEANS THE BATTER IS TO HIT STRAIGHT AWAY, BUT IF I PUT THEM ON MY HIPS, THEN HE OR SHE IS TO BUNT...

IF I WALK UP AND DOWN IN THE COACHING BOX, IT MEANS FOR THE BATTER TO WAIT OUT THE PITCHER.. IN OTHER WORDS, TO TRY FOR A WALK....

BUT NOW, AFTER ALL IS SAID AND DONE, IT MUST BE ADMITTED THAT SIGNALS ALONE NEVER WON A BALL GAME...

IT'S THE SPIRIT OF THE TEAM THAT COUNTS! THE **INTEREST** THAT THE PLAYERS SHOW IN THEIR TEAM! AM I RIGHT?

I SAID, AM I RIGHT?

3-27

YOU'RE RIGHT... ✳ SIGH ✳

4-10

SCHROEDER, IF I TOLD YOU THAT I HAD THE FEELING YOU AND I WOULD GET MARRIED SOMEDAY, WOULD YOU CHUCKLE LIGHTLY OR LAUGH LOUD AND LONG?

I DON'T KNOW...IT'S KIND OF HARD TO SAY OFFHAND...

4-17

SCHROEDER, I HAVE THE FEELING THAT YOU AND I WILL GET MARRIED SOMEDAY...

HA HA HA HAHAHA

HOHOHOHO HAHAHAHA

HE'D LAUGH LOUD AND LONG!

PEANUTS by Schulz

SCHROEDER STILL MAKES THE BEST CATCHER WE'VE EVER HAD, AND "PIG-PEN" DOES WELL AT THIRD BASE..

OUR OUTFIELD COULD BE BETTER, BUT IT'S THE BEST WE CAN DO, I GUESS...

WHAT I'M LOOKING FOR IS A GOOD SHORTSTOP-SECOND BASE COMBINATION... TWO GUYS WHO CAN REALLY WORK THOSE DOUBLE-PLAYS...

WAPP!

CLOMP!

PFUTT!

I THINK I'VE FOUND IT!

4-24

SCHULZ

**ZOING!**

5-1

Tm. Reg. U. S. Pat. Off.—All rights reserved
Copr. 1960 by United Feature Syndicate, Inc.

WHAT A STRUGGLE...IT TOOK ME FORTY-FIVE MINUTES TO LAND HIM!

OKAY, CHARLIE BROWN...LET'S GIVE HIM THE OL' FAST ONE... LET'S THROW IT RIGHT BY HIM!

HMPF!

WELL, WHAT ELSE CAN WE USE FOR HOME PLATE?

PEANUTS by SCHULZ

 CRUNCH! CHOMP! CRUNCH!

 WHAT IN THE WORLD ARE YOU EATING?

 CRUNCH CHOMP CHOMP CHOMP CRUNCH SMACK

 SUGAR LUMPS WITH HONEY!

5-15

 CRUNCH CRUNCH CHOMP CHOMP CRUNCH CHOMP CHOMP

 THEY'RE GOOD WITH CINNAMON, TOO!

SCHULZ

SKRITCH
SKRITCH
SKRITCH

SKRITCH
SKRITCH
SKRITCH

SIGH

MMMMMM?

SKRITCH SKRITCH
SKRITCH SKRITCH

SIGH

5-22

ENCORE!

SCHULZ

Tm. Reg. U. S. Pat. Off.—All rights reserved
Copr. 1960 by United Feature Syndicate, Inc.

TYRANNOSAURUS REX! LIFE SIZE, FIFTY FEET LONG AND TWENTY FEET HIGH! WOW!

MODEL SIZE...SIXTEEN INCHES LONG AND TEN INCHES HIGH...

HE SURE HAD A LOT OF BONES...

A DINOSAUR SET! OH, BOY! MAY I HELP YOU PUT HIM TOGETHER, LUCY?

OH, I SUPPOSE SO...

THIS LOOKS REAL INTERESTING.. THERE'S SOMETHING ABOUT DINOSAURS THAT'S FASCINATING.

LET'S SEE NOW...THIS TOE BONE HERE SHOULD CONNECT TO THIS FOOT BONE...

UH HUH...RIGHT...AND THIS FOOT BONE HERE SHOULD CONNECT TO THIS ANKLE BONE...

AND THE ANKLE BONE CONNECTS TO THE LEG BONE! **RIGHT?**

OH, THE ANKLE BONE CONNECTS TO THE LEG BONE...AND THE LEG BONE CONNECTS TO THE THIGH BONE!

THE THIGH BONE CONNECTS TO THE HIP BONE AND THE HIP BONE CONNECTS TO THE KNEE BONE

6-5

OH, THE KNEE BONE CONNECTS TO THE WRIST BONE...

AND THE WRIST BONE CONNECTS TO THE.....

PEANUTS by SCHULZ

DO YOU THINK THE BIRDS APPRECIATE THESE HOUSES WE MAKE, CHARLIE BROWN?

I CAN'T SAY, ALTHOUGH I LIKE TO THINK THAT THEY DO..

WE NEED SOME SMOOTHER BOARDS..A FEW OF THESE PIECES ARE PRETTY ROUGH...

AAUGH!

?

A SLIVER! A SLIVER! I GOT A SLIVER IN MY FINGER!!!

YOU'D BETTER GO HOME, AND HAVE YOUR MOTHER TAKE IT OUT..

IT'LL HURT! IT'LL HURT! IT'LL HURT! SHE'LL STICK ME WITH A NEEDLE!! IT'LL HURT!!

OF COURSE, IT'LL HURT, BUT YOU DON'T WANT IT TO GET **INFECTED**, DO YOU?

I CAN'T STAND PAIN, CHARLIE BROWN!

LOOK, DO WHAT I DO..WHILE YOUR MOTHER IS TRYING TO GET THE SLIVER OUT, YOU PRETEND YOU'RE BEING TORTURED BY PIRATES WHO WANT YOU TO TELL THEM WHERE THE GOLD IS BURIED

6-26

SEE HOW BRAVE YOU CAN BE..

Tm. Reg. U. S. Pat Off.—All rights reserved
Copr. 1960 by United Feature Syndicate, Inc.

AUGH

I TOLD THEM WHERE THE GOLD WAS BURIED!

PARDON ME..

GOOD GRIEF!

THANK YOU VERY MUCH

Tm. Reg. U. S. Pat Off.—All rights reserved
Copr. 1960 by United Feature Syndicate, Inc.

7-3

IT JUST DOESN'T PAY TO LIVE TOO CLOSE TO THE BALL PARK!

7-17

LINUS! DON'T TELL ME YOU'RE RUNNING AWAY FROM HOME?!

YOU'RE **CRAZY!!** THEY **KNOW** YOU'RE BLUFFING! YOU'LL JUST MAKE A **FOOL** OUT OF YOURSELF!

YOU'LL HAVE TO GO BACK HOME THIS EVENING, AND THEN YOU'LL HAVE TO LISTEN TO YOUR MOTHER AND DAD TELL EVERYONE ABOUT HOW YOU TRIED TO RUN AWAY, AND YOU WERE SO CUTE AND SO SERIOUS AND THEY'LL ALL LAUGH!

IT JUST DOESN'T DO ANY **GOOD**! THEY'RE WAY AHEAD OF YOU!

IN OTHER WORDS, YOU CAN'T FIGHT CITY HALL!

THAT'S RIGHT!

NOW, GO ON HOME AND FORGET THE WHOLE THING..

✳WHEW✳ I WAS SCARED TO DEATH SOMEONE WASN'T GOING TO COME ALONG AND TALK ME OUT OF IT!

WAMM!

WUMM! ⚡ OOF ⚡

PONG!

WELL, HOW DID THE BOXING GO?

NOT SO GOOD... I GOT BEATEN..

REALLY? WHAT WAS IT THAT BEAT YOU? WAS IT A LEFT OR A RIGHT?

I DON'T KNOW...

WHEN YOU STOP TO THINK ABOUT IT, IT'S KIND OF HARD TO SAY!

7-31

THIS IS TERRIBLE...I JUST CAN'T GET TO SLEEP!

TM. Reg. U. S. Pat. Off.—All rights reserved
Copr. 1960 by United Feature Syndicate, Inc.

THERE'S NOTHING WORSE THAN BEING TIRED, AND YET BEING...BEING....

8-7

Z

Z

BOING!

..WIDE AWAKE!

SCHULZ

PEANUTS by Schulz

Panel 1: AREN'T THE CLOUDS BEAUTIFUL? THEY LOOK LIKE BIG BALLS OF COTTON...

Panel 2: I COULD JUST LIE HERE ALL DAY, AND WATCH THEM DRIFT BY...

Panel 3: IF YOU USE YOUR IMAGINATION, YOU CAN SEE LOTS OF THINGS IN THE CLOUD FORMATIONS... WHAT DO YOU THINK YOU SEE, LINUS?

Panel 4: WELL, THOSE CLOUDS UP THERE LOOK TO ME LIKE THE MAP OF THE BRITISH HONDURAS ON THE CARIBBEAN..

Panel 5: THAT CLOUD UP THERE LOOKS A LITTLE LIKE THE PROFILE OF THOMAS EAKINS, THE FAMOUS PAINTER AND SCULPTOR...

Panel 6: AND THAT GROUP OF CLOUDS OVER THERE GIVES ME THE IMPRESSION OF THE STONING OF STEPHEN... I CAN SEE THE APOSTLE PAUL STANDING THERE TO ONE SIDE...

Panel 7: UH HUH... THAT'S VERY GOOD... WHAT DO YOU SEE IN THE CLOUDS, CHARLIE BROWN?

8-14

Panel 8: WELL, I WAS GOING TO SAY I SAW A DUCKY AND A HORSIE, BUT I CHANGED MY MIND!

SCHULZ

WHAT ARE YOU FOLLOWING ME AROUND FOR ?!

AM I SUPPOSED TO BE HONORED BY YOUR PRESENCE ?

GO ON! GET OUT OF HERE! WHAT MAKES YOU THINK EVERYBODY WANTS YOU AROUND ALL THE TIME ?!

SHE'S RIGHT...I MUST MAKE AN AWFUL NUISANCE OF MYSELF SOMETIMES...

SNOOPY!

OH, I'M SO GLAD TO SEE YOU! JUST KNOWING YOU'RE AROUND ALWAYS MAKES ME FEEL GOOD!

9-18

Tm. Reg. U. S. Pat. Off.—All rights reserved
Copr. 1960 by United Feature Syndicate, Inc.

BLAH

SCHULZ

# Other *Snoopy* books published by Ravette

## Colour landscapes in this series

| | |
|---|---|
| Be Prepared | £2.95 |
| Stay Cool | £2.95 |
| Shall We Dance? | £2.95 |
| Let's Go | £2.95 |
| Come Fly With Me | £2.95 |

## Black and white landscapes

| | |
|---|---|
| It's a Dog's Life | £2.50 |
| Roundup | £2.50 |
| Freewheelin' | £2.50 |
| Joe Cool | £2.50 |
| Dogs Don't Eat Dessert | £2.50 |
| You're on the Wrong Foot Again, Charlie Brown | £2.50 |

All these books are available at your local bookshop or newsagent, or can be ordered direct from the publisher. Just tick the titles you require and fill in the form below. Prices and availability subject to change without notice.

Ravette Limited, 3 Glenside Estate, Star Road, Partridge Green, Horsham, West Sussex RH13 8RA

Please send a cheque or postal order, and allow the following for postage and packing. UK: 45p for one book plus 30p for each additional book.

Name ................................................................

Address ............................................................

............................................................